The NFL's Greatest Teams

New Orleans Saints

Big Buddy Books
An Imprint of Abdo Publishing
www.abdopublishing.com

Marcia Zappa

www.abdopublishing.com

Published by Abdo Publishing, a division of ABDO, PO Box 398166, Minneapolis, Minnesota 55439.
Copyright © 2015 by Abdo Consulting Group, Inc. International copyrights reserved in all countries. No part
of this book may be reproduced in any form without written permission from the publisher. Big Buddy Books™
is a trademark and logo of Abdo Publishing.

Printed in the United States of America, North Mankato, Minnesota.
092014
012015

Cover Photo: ASSOCIATED PRESS.
Interior Photos: ASSOCIATED PRESS (pp. 7, 9, 13, 15, 17, 19, 20, 21, 24, 25, 27, 28, 29); Getty Images (pp. 5,
   7, 9, 18, 19, 20); NFL (p. 11); Klaus Nowottnick/picture-alliance/dpa/AP Images (p. 23); Sports Illustrated/
   Getty Images (p. 25).

Coordinating Series Editor: Rochelle Baltzer
Contributing Editors: Megan M. Gunderson, Sarah Tieck
Graphic Design: Michelle Labatt

Library of Congress Cataloging-in-Publication Data

Zappa, Marcia, 1985-
  New Orleans Saints / Marcia Zappa.
     pages cm. -- (The NFL's Greatest Teams)
  Audience: Age: 7-11.
  ISBN 978-1-62403-588-3
1. New Orleans Saints (Football team)--History--Juvenile literature. I. Title.
  GV956.N366Z37 2015
  796.332'640976335--dc23
                      2014026421

Contents

A Winning Team

The New Orleans Saints are a football team from New Orleans, Louisiana. They have played in the National Football League (NFL) for more than 45 years.

The Saints have had good seasons and bad. But over the years, they've proven themselves. Let's see what makes the Saints one of the NFL's greatest teams.

Gold, black, and white are the team's colors.

5

League Play

Team Standings

The NFC and the American Football Conference (AFC) make up the NFL. Each conference has a north, south, east, and west division.

The NFL got its start in 1920. Its teams have changed over the years. Today, there are 32 teams. They make up two conferences and eight divisions.

The Saints play in the South Division of the National Football Conference (NFC). This division also includes the Atlanta Falcons, the Carolina Panthers, and the Tampa Bay Buccaneers.

The Falcons are a major rival of the Saints.
Fans get excited when they face off!

Kicking Off

Name Game

November 1 is a holiday called All Saints' Day. The team chose to form on this day because it references the team's name.

The Saints became a team on November 1, 1966. New Orleans is famous for **jazz** music. The name *Saints* comes from the jazz song "When the Saints Go Marching In."

The team began play in 1967. Like many new teams, the Saints struggled at first. In fact, they didn't have a winning season for their first 20 years!

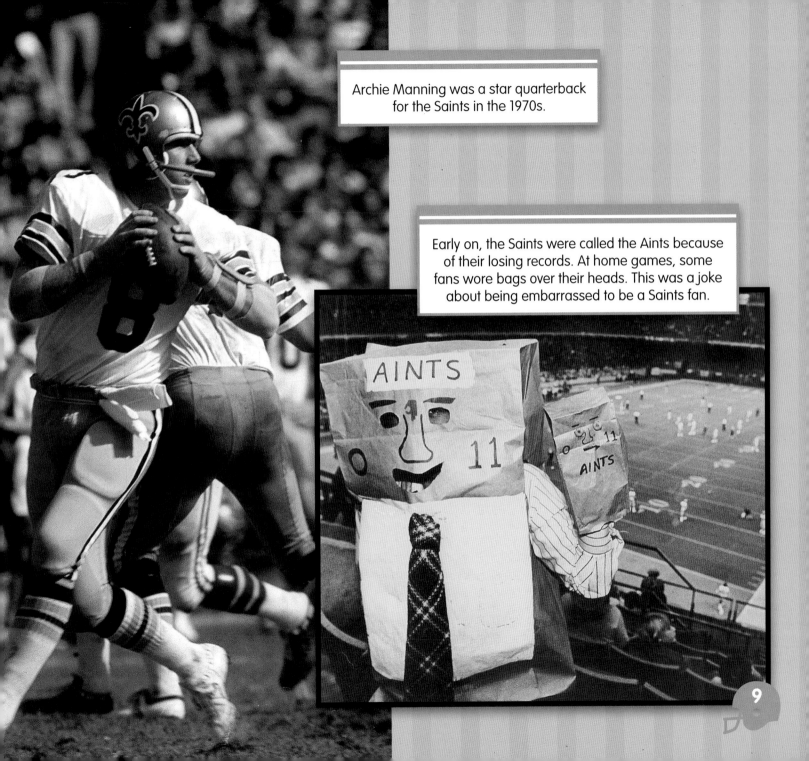

Archie Manning was a star quarterback for the Saints in the 1970s.

Early on, the Saints were called the Aints because of their losing records. At home games, some fans wore bags over their heads. This was a joke about being embarrassed to be a Saints fan.

Highlight Reel

In 1987, the Saints had their first winning season. They made it to the play-offs. But, they lost the first play-off game to the Minnesota Vikings 44–10.

The Saints made it back to the play-offs in 1990, 1991, and 1992. But each time, they lost the first game.

The Saints returned to the play-offs in 2000. They beat the Saint Louis Rams for their first play-off win!

In 2000, the Saints beat the Rams 31–28 in their first game of the play-offs.

In 2006, head coach Sean Payton took over the Saints. He and quarterback Drew Brees led the team to its first NFC **championship** game. But, they lost to the Chicago Bears 39–14.

The Saints continued their strong play over the next few seasons. In 2010, they appeared in their first Super Bowl. They beat the Indianapolis Colts 31–17!

Drew Brees was named the Most Valuable Player (MVP) of the 2010 Super Bowl.

Halftime! Stat Break

Team Records

RUSHING YARDS
Career: Deuce McAllister, 6,096 yards (2001–2008)
Single Season: George Rogers, 1,674 yards (1981)

PASSING YARDS
Career: Drew Brees, 38,733 yards and gaining (2006–)
Single Season: Drew Brees, 5,476 yards (2011)

RECEPTIONS
Career: Marques Colston, 607 receptions (2006–2013)
Single Season: Jimmy Graham, 99 receptions (2011)

ALL-TIME LEADING SCORER
Morten Andersen, 1,318 points (1982–1994)

Famous Coaches

Jim Mora (1986–1996)
Sean Payton (2006–2011, 2013–)

Championships

SUPER BOWL APPEARANCES:
2010

SUPER BOWL WINS:
2010

Fan Fun

STADIUM: Mercedes-Benz Superdome
LOCATION: New Orleans, Louisiana
MASCOTS: Sir Saint (*left*) and
Gumbo (*right*)

Pro Football Hall of Famers & Their Years with the Saints

Jim Finks, Administrator (1986–1992)
Rickey Jackson, Linebacker (1981–1993)
Willie Roaf, Tackle (1993–2001)

Coaches' Corner

Jim Mora became head coach of the Saints in 1986. The next year, he led the team to its first winning season and play-off appearance. He was named the NFL's Coach of the Year.

Sean Payton took over the Saints in 2006. He has led the team to many play-offs. And, he led them to a win in their first Super Bowl!

Mora coached the Saints for 11 seasons.

Before Payton became head coach, the Saints had only won one play-off game. After Payton took over, they won five play-off games and a Super Bowl!

17

Star Players

Archie Manning
QUARTERBACK
(1971–1975, 1977–1982)

Archie Manning was the team's first choice in the 1971 **draft**. As starting quarterback, he led the team for many years. He set several passing records for the Saints. In 1998, Manning became one of the first members of the Superdome Wall of Fame.

Rickey Jackson LINEBACKER (1981–1993)

Rickey Jackson quickly became a star player by getting eight sacks during his **rookie** season. In 1987, he helped the Saints have their first winning season and make it to the play-offs for the first time. As a Saint, Jackson had 123 sacks. That is a team record. Jackson became a member of the Pro Football Hall of Fame in 2010.

Morten Andersen KICKER (1982–1994)

Morten Andersen kicked for the Saints for 13 seasons. During this time, he scored 1,318 points. That is more than any other Saint. Andersen was known for being **accurate**. He was so reliable he was called "Mr. Automatic." He was chosen to play in the Pro Bowl, which is the NFL's all-star game, six times as a Saint.

Eric Martin WIDE RECEIVER (1985–1993)

Eric Martin was a late **draft** pick for the Saints in 1985. But, he soon surprised the team and fans with his skill. During his time with the Saints, Martin had 532 receptions for 7,854 yards. That was a team record for many years.

Willie Roaf TACKLE (1993–2001)

Willie Roaf was the team's first pick in the 1993 draft. He was a strong tackle. In 2000, Roaf helped the team get its first play-off win. He was selected to play in the Pro Bowl seven times as a Saint. Roaf became a member of the Pro Football Hall of Fame in 2012.

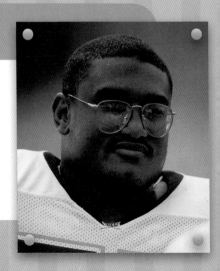

Deuce McAllister RUNNING BACK (2001–2008)

Deuce McAllister played for the Saints his whole **career**. He was known for his power and speed. McAllister rushed for 6,096 yards during his career. That is more than any other Saint. And, he has more rushing touchdowns than any other Saint, with 49.

Drew Brees QUARTERBACK (2006–)

Drew Brees joined the Saints in 2006. During his first season, he helped the team reach the NFC **championship** for the first time. In 2010, he led the team to a win in its first Super Bowl! Brees has broken many team and NFL passing records.

The Superdome

The Saints play home games at the Mercedes-Benz Superdome. It is in New Orleans. The Superdome opened in 1975. It is the largest domed football stadium in the United States. It can hold more than 73,000 people.

The Superdome hosted the Super Bowl for the seventh time in 2013.

23

Who Dat?

Fans flock to the Superdome to see the Saints play home games. They are known for their loud "Who Dat" **chant**.

The team's **mascots** are Gumbo and Sir Saint. They help fans cheer on the team at home games.

Saints fans are often called the Who Dat Nation.

Singing Saints

The "Who Dat" chant became popular after a song was released by fan Steve Monistere in 1983. The song featured singer Aaron Neville and several Saints players.

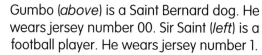

Gumbo (*above*) is a Saint Bernard dog. He wears jersey number 00. Sir Saint (*left*) is a football player. He wears jersey number 1.

Final Call

The Saints have a long, rich history. Starting out, they struggled for many years. But in 2010, they became Super Bowl **champions**.

Even during losing seasons, true fans have stuck by them. Many believe the New Orleans Saints will remain one of the greatest teams in the NFL.

Saints fans are hopeful that their team will continue to succeed.

Through the Years

1966

The Saints become the 16th team in the NFL.

1967

The team plays its first game on September 17. They lose to the Los Angeles Rams 27–13.

1970

Tom Dempsey makes a 63-yard field goal. It was an NFL record for many years.

1975

The Superdome opens. Before this, the team played home games at Tulane Stadium.

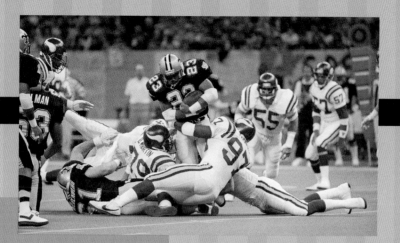

1987

The team has its first winning season. They make it to the play-offs for the first time.

2005

Hurricane Katrina destroys New Orleans. The team begins playing home games in other cities.

2006

The team plays in the NFC **championship** for the first time. They lose to the Chicago Bears 39–14.

2010

The Saints play in their first Super Bowl. They beat the Indianapolis Colts 31–17.

Postgame Recap

1. How long did the Saints play before having a winning season?
   A. 1 year   **B**. 10 years   **C**. 20 years

2. What is the name of the stadium where the Saints play home games?
   A. NOLA Stadium
   B. Mercedes-Benz Superdome
   C. Saints Superdome

3. Name 1 of the 3 Saints in the Pro Football Hall of Fame.

4. Where did the Saints get their name?
   A. The song "When the Saints Go Marching In"
   B. The popular religious saints of New Orleans
   C. Their first owner, George Saint

Glossary

accurate free from mistakes.

career a period of time spent in a certain job.

champion the winner of a championship, which is a game, a match, or a race held to find a first-place winner.

chant a word or a phrase that is repeated to a beat. Usually, chants are spoken loudly by a crowd.

draft a system for professional sports teams to choose new players. When a team drafts a player, they choose that player for their team.

jazz a form of American music that features lively and unusual beats. It first became popular in the early 1900s.

mascot something to bring good luck and help cheer on a team.

rookie a first-year player in a professional sport.

Websites

To learn more about the NFL's Greatest Teams, visit **booklinks.abdopublishing.com**. These links are routinely monitored and updated to provide the most current information available.

Index